The World of HORSES
LUSITANOS

Lorijo Metz

PowerKiDS
press
New York

To Kay Laake, IALHA, V.P. and to Lisa Diersen and Dr. Nancy Holman from
The Royal Lusitano Farm in St. Charles, Illinois

Published in 2013 by The Rosen Publishing Group, Inc.
29 East 21st Street, New York, NY 10010

Editor: Amelie von Zumbusch
Book Design: Kate Laczynski

Photo Credits: Back cover graphic (big horseshoe) © www.iStockphoto.com/Deborah Cheramie; back cover graphic (background horseshoes) Purematterian/Shutterstock.com; cover, p. 6 Claudia Steininger/Shutterstock.com; pp. 4–5, 10, 12 by Karl Knapp; p. 7 (top) Makarova Viktoria (Vikarus)/Shutterstock.com; pp. 7 (bottom), 16 by Nancy N. Holman @ The Royal Lusitano; p. 8 Paulo De Oliveira/Taxi/Getty Images; p. 9 by Laura McClure Photography; pp. 11, 13 by Lisa Diersen; p. 14 iStockphoto/Thinkstock; p. 15 Jean-Luc Manaud/Contributor/Gamma-Rapho/Getty Images; p. 17 David Hecker/Staff/AFP/Getty Images; p. 18 (top) Joe Patronite/Riser/Getty Images; p. 18 (bottom) Panoramic Images/Getty Images; p. 19 Francisco Leong/Stringer/AFP/Getty Images; p. 20 © NaturePL/SuperStock; p. 21 Janek Skarzynski/Staff/AFP/Getty Images; p. 22 by JC Andalusians.

Library of Congress Cataloging-in-Publication Data
Metz, Lorijo.
  Lusitanos / by Lorijo Metz. — 1st ed.
    p. cm. — (The world of horses)
  Includes index.
  ISBN 978-1-4488-7430-9 (library binding) — ISBN 978-1-4488-7503-0 (pbk.) —
ISBN 978-1-4488-7577-1 (6-pack)
  1. Lusitano horse—Juvenile literature. I. Title.
  SF293.L5M485 2013
  636.1'38—dc23
                                    2011051872

Manufactured in China

CPSIA Compliance Information: Batch #WKTS12PK: For Further Information contact Rosen Publishing, New York, New York at 1-800-237-9932

Contents

Brave Lusitanos 4

What Do Lusitanos Look Like? 6

Strong and Skilled... 8

Caring for Lusitanos 10

Lusitano Foals.. 12

History of the Lusitano 14

Dressage 16

Portuguese Bullfighting 18

Lusitanos Today 20

The Future of Lusitanos 22

Glossary 23

Index 24

Websites.. 24

Lusitano horses are famous for facing angry bulls in the bullring while carrying riders, called *cavaleiros*. When the bulls charge, the horses do not move until the last possible moment. A horse must be both brave and calm to face a charging bull. It must also be quick. Lusitanos are all these things and more.

> The Lusitano is also known as the Puro Sangue Lusitano. This means "pure-blooded Lusitano" in Portuguese. It is sometimes shortened to "PSL."

Lusitanos come from horses that lived on the Iberian Peninsula over 22,000 years ago. They take their name from Lusitania, an ancient Roman province that covered part of the peninsula. Most of Lusitania is now in Portugal, the country from which Lusitanos come.

5

Lusitanos have long, noble heads and curved noses. They have long, silky manes and tails. To make them easier to care for, Lusitano owners often keep the manes and tails of younger horses and mares clipped short.

Horses are measured in hands. One hand equals 4 inches (10 cm). Lusitanos stand 15 to 16 hands high from the ground to the tops of their **withers**, or shoulders.

Lusitanos are known for their large, almond-shaped eyes.

Lusitanos have medium-sized ears.

This Lusitano is gray. Gray horses often look white. However, the skin beneath their coats is always black.

Most Lusitanos are gray. A few are other colors such as bay, or reddish brown with black **points**, and palomino, or tan with white points. Points are a horse's mane, tail, and lower legs.

7

Strong and Skilled

Lusitanos have strong necks set on sturdy shoulders and backs. They have powerful **hindquarters**, or hips, and long legs.

Like Lipizzans and Andalusian horses, Lusitanos do well in the sport of **dressage**, which involves years of training to master advanced

Though they are strong and brave, Lusitanos are also very gentle.

movements. Good dressage horses are usually strong, graceful, and have good balance. Lusitanos have these features because they started out as warhorses. In the past, people used horses when fighting wars. Warhorses needed to be strong but remain calm in the face of battle. They also had to be hardworking and easy to work with.

Caring for Lusitanos

Lusitanos are hot-blooded, or spirited, horses. They need fresh air and daily exercise. They also need their own **stalls** filled with clean straw in a barn or stable.

Owners must treat Lusitanos' silky manes and tails with care. They often braid them to keep them clean and prevent tangling. A person called a

This Lusitano's mane has been braided to keep it neat.

This Lusitano is grazing, or eating grass in a field.

farrier will trim Lusitanos' hooves and replace horseshoes as needed. At least once a year, Lusitanos should see a **veterinarian**, or animal doctor.

Lusitanos eat hay and grains like oats and barley. They also need plenty of fresh water and should have a block of salt to lick.

Lusitano Foals

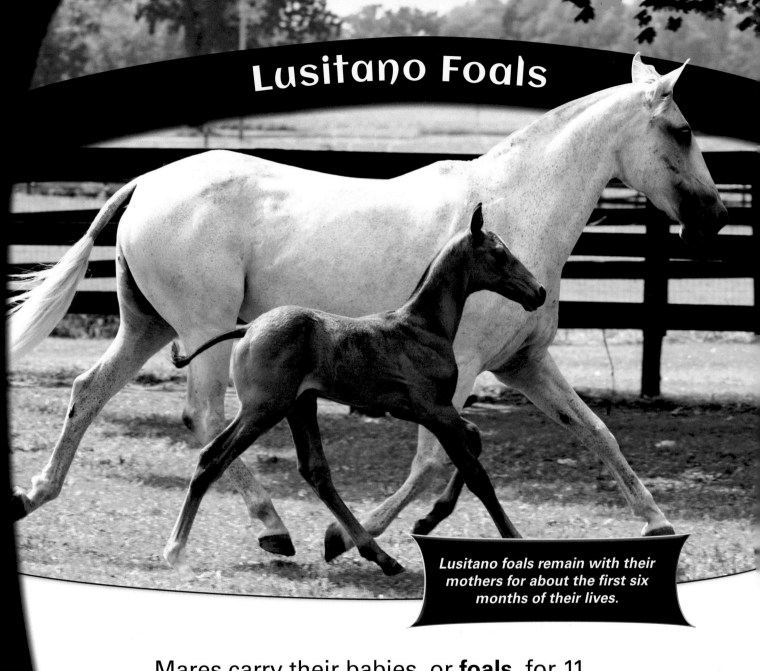

Lusitano foals remain with their mothers for about the first six months of their lives.

Mares carry their babies, or **foals**, for 11 months. Newborns weigh between 65 and 75 pounds (29–34 kg). They are most often brown or black. Over the next eight to nine years, most Lusitanos will turn gray.

Shortly after they are born, foals can stand. They run within hours of their birth. Lusitanos grow more slowly than other **breeds**, or types, of horses. Their training starts early, though. This early training is called groundwork. Foals do not work under saddle, meaning they are not ridden, until they are at least three years old. Lusitanos live for between 30 and 35 years.

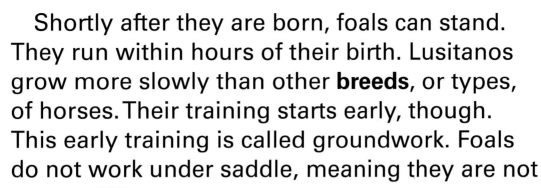

Lusitano foals are born with long legs. In fact, a foal's legs are nearly as long as an adult's.

Portugal and Spain are part of the Iberian Peninsula. Their horses share a common history. For most of it, they were all called Iberian or Andalusian horses. Thousands of years ago, ancient Greeks landed on the Iberian Peninsula. They were amazed by the speed of Iberian riders and their horses. In time, they introduced a

This is an Andalusian. As you can see, it looks a lot like a Lusitano.

This is the royal stud farm in Alter do Chão, Portugal. Horses have been bred there for hundreds of years. The horses from the stud farm make up the Alter Real branch of Lusitanos.

style of riding that was used in battle and later in bullfighting. In the seventeenth century, the Spanish stopped using horses in bullfighting, while the Portuguese continued.

Over time, Andalusians raised in Spain became different from those raised in Portugal. In 1966, the breed split. The Portuguese horses became known as Lusitanos.

15

Dressage

Lusitanos compete in dressage in many **equestrian**, or horse, events. In dressage, horses perform advanced moves that are almost like a dance. There are dressage events at the Olympics and the World Equestrian Games. Luiza Tavares de Almeida, a 16-year-old from Brazil, rode a Lusitano in a dressage competition at the 2008 Olympics. She became the youngest rider to take part in the Olympics.

In dressage, the horse and rider work closely together. Horses must have grace as well as strength. Training takes years.

Along with Lipizzans and Andalusians, Lusitanos are known for performing the advanced leaps and jumps known as the airs above the ground. While these movements are not used in competition, they are performed at horse shows and other events.

Portuguese Bullfighting

Bullfighting began as a way for men and horses trained in war to use their skills during peacetime. In Portuguese bullfighting, cavaleiros do not kill the bull.

A Portuguese bullfight begins with a parade of cavaleiros and horses. The

The Campo Pequeno Bullring, seen here, is in Portugal's capital city, Lisbon.

Women also ride in Portuguese bullfights. They are known as cavaleiras.

Here, Portuguese cavaleiro Luis Miguel da Veiga takes part in a bullfight.

horses go through the airs above the ground. After that, one rider and horse remain and a bull enters the ring. The cavaleiro and horse use their skills to get close enough to place several darts in the bull. When the bull charges, the cavaleiro waits until the last possible moment to command the horse to step out of the way.

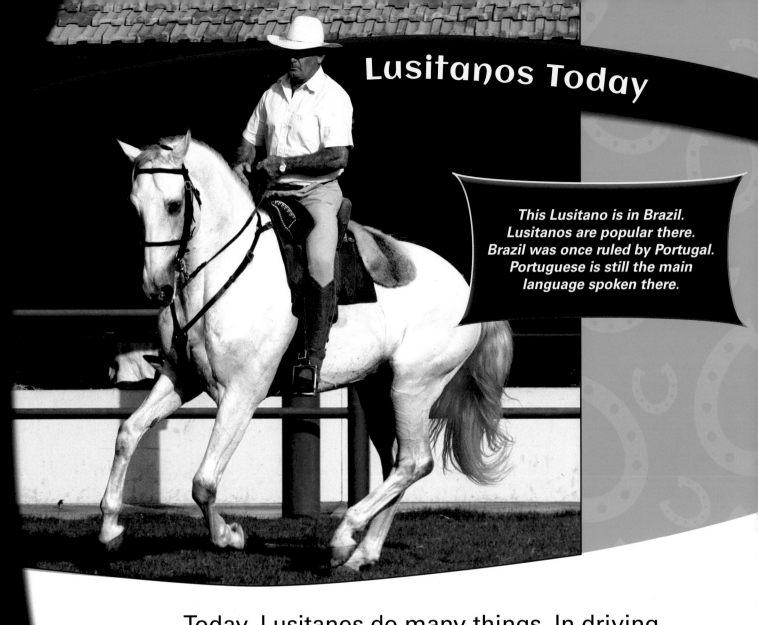

Lusitanos Today

This Lusitano is in Brazil. Lusitanos are popular there. Brazil was once ruled by Portugal. Portuguese is still the main language spoken there.

Today, Lusitanos do many things. In driving events, teams of Lusitanos pull wagons or carriages. For these events, they must wear **tack**. Tack is the gear horses wear over their heads to connect them to the carriage. It includes long straps, called **reins**, which drivers use to control the horses.

In Great Britain, Lusitanos have proven themselves to be Olympic-level show jumpers. In South America, the people who round up cattle often ride Lusitanos. Their calm, gentle nature also makes Lusitanos perfect for **therapeutic riding**. In therapeutic riding, people who have trouble walking or are disabled in some other way learn to ride.

Lusitanos are good horses for riders who perform riding stunts. The stunt rider Lorenzo the Flying Frenchman performs with a team of Lusitanos.

Working equitation is among the fastest-growing equestrian events at the International Festival of Purebred Lusitano Horses, in Cascais, Portugal. In it, horses and riders wear the styles of tack and clothes from their countries. The horses and riders prove their skills in everything from dressage to herding cows.

Lusitanos are admired both in Portugal and around the world.

In recent years, Lusitanos have become more popular. These horses are now raised in many places, from Interagro Farm, in Itapira, Brazil, to the Royal Lusitanos, in St. Charles, Illinois.

Glossary

breeds (BREEDZ) Groups of animals that look alike and have the same relatives.

cavaleiros (kah-vah-LAY-roos) People who ride horses in Portuguese-style bullfighting.

dressage (dreh-SAZH) Dance-like movements that horses are trained to do.

equestrian (ih-KWES-tree-un) Having to do with riding horses.

farrier (FER-ee-er) A person who puts shoes on horses.

foals (FOHLZ) Young horses.

hindquarters (HYND-kwahr-terz) The back part of an animal.

points (POYNTS) A horse's mane, tail, and lower legs.

reins (RAYNZ) Strips that attach to a bridle or bit and are used to direct an animal.

stalls (STOLZ) Spots for animals in a barn or stable.

tack (TAK) The gear used to ride or drive a horse.

therapeutic riding (ther-uh-PYOO-tik RY-ding) A method of riding for people with special needs that aims to heal or help them.

veterinarian (veh-tuh-ruh-NER-ee-un) A doctor who treats animals.

withers (WIH-therz) A place between the shoulders of a dog or horse.

Index

B
breed(s), 13, 15
bull(s), 4, 18–19

C
cavaleiro(s), 4, 18–19

D
dressage, 8, 16, 22

E
events, 16–17, 20, 22

F
farrier, 10

H
heads, 6, 20

hindquarters, 8

I
Iberian Peninsula, 4, 14

L
Lusitania, 4

M
mane(s), 6–7, 10

N
name, 4
noses, 6

P
points, 7

Portugal, 4, 14–15, 22

R
reins, 20

S
stalls, 10

T
tack, 20, 22
tail(s), 6–7, 10
therapeutic riding, 21

V
veterinarian, 11

W
withers, 6

Websites

Due to the changing nature of Internet links, PowerKids Press has developed an online list of websites related to the subject of this book. This site is updated regularly. Please use this link to access the list: www.powerkidslinks.com/woh/lus/